Getting Results by Prayer
You Must Be Born Again
The Great Adventure

EMMET FOX

CHURCH OF THE HEALING CHRIST
Biltmore Hotel - New York

15 CENTS

These three essays are printed together because they supplement each other. Each one deals with a vital aspect of spiritual demonstration.—E. F.

Getting Results by Prayer

GREAT deal of confusion seems to exist in many minds concerning the precise avenue through which the Divine Power is to be approached, and realization and harmony attained. So many schools of thought seem to be competing for the attention of the student; so busy is the printing press; so many new books and pamphlets are written; so many magazines come and go; that people have told me that they have felt quite in despair of ever discovering what it really is that they must do to be saved.

Sometimes it seems as though the story of Babel were repeating itself in the metaphysical movement—and yet we all know in our hearts that the true Gate is narrow and the real Way strait. One well known Eastern teacher of great spiritual power has actually published a pamphlet from which it appears that the genuine criterion of authenticity is to have no Path at all. This is the *reductio ad absurdum* which pulls us up short and restores the light.

The truth, of course, is this, that the only solution of the problem is definitely to contact the Divine Power which dwells within your own soul; and, having consciously done that, to bring it to bear upon the various difficulties in your life, taking them in due order, that is, attacking the most urgent first. This is the right way of working, and it is the only way that can possibly help you, or your affairs, in the long run. The real remedy for every one of your difficulties is, as we are told on every page of the Bible, to find and *know* the Indwelling Presence. *Acquaint now thyself with Him and be at peace. In His Presence is fulness of joy. Behold, I am with you alway.*

This, then, is the task, and the only one— to find, and consciously know, your own Indwelling Lord.

You see now how the confusion disappears, melts away, and the perfect simplicity of the whole thing emerges once you realize this fact. From this it necessarily follows that all schools and churches; all teachers, under whatever name they may be called; all the textbooks, magazines, pamphlets, and what-not; are but temporary expedients for enabling you to make this contact. In themselves they are of no importance except as a means to an end. The best mode of approach to Divine things for you is the one that happens to make it easiest for you to locate the Inner Light within yourself.

Such things as temperament, education, family tradition, and so on, will make one book, or one teacher, or one school, more useful than another; but never as anything more than the means to a certain end. That end is effective self discovery. "Man know *thyself*"—thy true self which is the Divine I Am. And so we see that the best "movement," the finest textbook, the greatest teacher, is just the one that happens best to fit the individual need. It is entirely a practical matter, and the only test that ever could, or ever will, be of any use, is the practical one of *judgment by results*. Of course, Jesus anticipated this difficulty, and met it, as he has met all our difficulties. He gave us the simple and perfect standard: *By their fruits ye shall know them.*

The great peril to true religion has always been the building up of vested interests in wealthy organizations, or in the exploitation by individuals of their own personalities. An organized church is always in danger of developing into an "industry" which has to provide a living for numerous officials. When this happens the rank and file are sure to be severely discouraged from seeking spiritual things for themselves at first hand. A tradition of "loyalty" to the organization is built up as a means of self protection. Not loyalty to Truth, or to your own soul, be it remarked, but to the ecclesiastical machine. Thus the means becomes an end in itself and spiritual power then fades out. Rash promises and vague claims take the place of real verifiable demonstrations.

In the case of leaders who exploit their own personalities, the student is discouraged from going elsewhere for enlightenment or help; and here again "loyalty" to something other than God is allowed to block the avenue of Truth, and therefore becomes antichrist. What is this but the jealousy of the petty tradesman who warns a doubtful customer of the danger he runs in going to the "shop next door."

Remember that you absolutely owe no loyalty whatever to anything or anyone but your own soul and to the furtherance of its spiritual development. Your most solemn duty is to make everything secondary to that. "To thine own self be true; and it must follow, as the night the day, thou canst not then be false to any man."—*Shakespeare*.

The first step that the earnest student must take is to settle on a definite method of working, selecting whichever one seems to suit him best, and then giving it a fair trial. That means that you must acquire a definite method or system of spiritual treatment or scientific prayer. Merely reading books, making good resolutions, or talking plausibly about the thing will get you nowhere. *Get a definite method of working,* practise it conscientiously every day; and stick to one method long enough to give it a fair chance. You would not expect to play the violin after two or three attempts, or to drive a car without a little preliminary practice.

Having got your method, set to work definitely on some concrete problem in your own life, choosing preferably whichever is causing you the most trouble at the moment, or, better still, *whatever it is that you are most afraid of.* Work at it steadily; and if nothing has happened, if no improvement at all shows itself within, say, a couple of weeks at the outside, then try it on another problem. If you still get no result, then scrap that method and adopt a new one. Remember, *there is a way out;* that is as certain as the rising of the sun. The problem really is, not the getting rid of your difficulties, but the finding of your own best method for do-ing it.

If ill health is your difficulty, do not rest until you have brought about at least one bodily healing. There is no malady that has not been healed by someone at some time, and what others have done you can do, for God is Principle, and Principle changes not.

If poverty is the trouble, go to work on that, and clear it up once and for all. It can be done. It has been done. Others have done it, and you can.

If you are unhappy, dissatisfied with your lot, or your surroundings, above all, with yourself, set to work on that; refuse to take no for an answer; and insist upon the hap-piness and satisfaction that are yours by Divine right.

If your need is self-expression—artistic, literary, or otherwise—if your heart's desire is to attain to eminence in a profession, or some kind of public career, that, too, ap-proached in the right spirit, is a legitimate and worthy object, and the right method of scientific prayer will bring you the prize.

Keep a record of your results, and on no account be satisfied with anything less than success. Above all things, avoid the deadly error of making excuses. There are no excuses for failing to demonstrate. When you do not demonstrate, it never by any chance means anything except that you have not worked in the right way. Excuses are the true and veritable devil, who comes to tempt you to remain outside the Kingdom of Heaven, while the Gate stands open. Excuses, in fact, are the only enemy that you really need to fear.

Find the method that suits you; cultivate simplicity—simplicity and spontaneity are the secret of effective prayer—work away steadily; *keep your own counsel;* and *whatsoever ye shall ask in My name, that will I do.*

You Must Be Born Again

WE are told concerning the teaching of Jesus that the common people heard him gladly. This could easily have been inferred from the most superficial study of the Gospels. The "man in the street," unsophisticated by theology or philosophy, has an intuitive perception of fundamental Truth when he meets it, that is often lacking in highly trained minds. Intellectual attainments may easily beget spiritual pride, and this is the only sin upon which Our Lord was severe. Yet among the learned, too, there were those, the more spiritually minded, who felt themselves attracted to the new Teacher. He was unconventional, hopelessly out of favor with the ecclesiastical authorities, a flouter of hallowed traditions; and yet, deep calleth unto deep, and so he had his friends and followers in high places also. One of these who felt irresistibly drawn to seek for further light

was Nicodemus. He had the thirst for
Divine things that will not be denied, but
moral courage was not his strong point, and
so he sought out the Teacher by night. That
he should have gone at all was proof of the
compelling power of the urge. Clearly the
unfoldment of his spiritual nature was, in
spite of defects in character, the principal
thing in his life, and clearly he was dissatisfied with the progress he was making.
Jesus, he believed, had something to give that
was vital, and that gift might be just the
secret that had hitherto eluded him, just the
key he needed to unlock the spiritual treasure-
house of his soul. Jesus might be able to
show him why he had so far failed to attain;
why, as we should say in modern phrase-
ology, he had failed to demonstrate. And
the Master's explanation was simple, concise,
almost overwhelming in its directness. He
said: *"You must be born again."*

This statement sums up the whole science
of demonstration as it is practised on the
spiritual basis. It is verily a textbook on

metaphysics compressed into five words. It
tells the whole story. You stand where you
do today, wherever that is, because you are
the man that you are. There is only one
way under heaven by which you can be
brought to stand anywhere else, and that is
by becoming another man. The man you are
cannot stand anywhere else; a different man
cannot stand where you are now. If you
wish to go up higher you can do so, and
there is no limit to the height which you can
attain upon that flight; but *you must be born
again!*

Why is it that we make so little progress,
compared, that is to say, with what we might
and should make in view of the knowledge
that we all, in this movement, possess—at
least in theory? Why do we not change day
by day and week by week from glory to
glory, until our friends can scarcely recog-
nize us for the same man or woman? Why
should we not march about the world looking
like gods, and feeling it; healing instanta-
neously all who come to us; reforming the

sinner; setting the captives free; and gener-
ally "doing the works"? "Who did hinder
you?"

And the reply is that demonstration, like
all other things, has its price; that the price
is that we be *born again,* and that in our
secret hearts, too often, that is a price that
we are not prepared to pay. We are in love
with the present man, and all the things that
constitute him, and we are not prepared to
slay him that the other may be born.

We come into Truth with our little finger,
and the great things will not come to us until
we come in with the entire body; and there's
the rub.

To come into Truth with your whole body
is to bring every conscious thought and belief
to the touchstone of Divine Intelligence and
Divine Love. It is to reject every single
thing, mental or physical, that does not
square with that standard. It is to revise
every opinion, every habit of thought, every
policy, every branch of practical conduct,
without any exception whatever.

This, of course, is something absolutely tremendous. It is no mere spring cleaning of the soul. It is nothing less than a wholesale tearing down and rebuilding of the entire house. Is it any wonder that all but the very strongest spirits shirk it. And yet, is it any wonder that without it one never really does get anywhere.

It means, as St. Paul said, "dying daily." It means parting with all the prejudices that you have inherited and acquired during all your life long. It means taking the knife to all the little faults of character, petty vanities, minor deceits, and all those lesser forms of selfishness and pride that crystallize your spiritual joints, and are so dear to you. It may mean giving up the biggest thing in your present life, but if it does—well, that is the price that must be paid, and that is all about it.

If you are not prepared to pay this price, well and good; but you must not expect to receive from the Law more than you pay for. A little finger in Truth is well, but it can only produce a little finger result. For a full-length demonstration the whole body must be full of light. *You must be born again.*

The Great Adventure

MANY people seem to have the impression that the sole object of Divine Science is the overcoming of difficulties; but to suppose that, is to lose all sense of proportion. The Truth is to be sought for its own sake. The knowledge of Truth is its own reward, and that reward is health, harmony, and prosperity, to begin with; but this is only the beginning. The real object of the seeker should be the development of his own higher faculties and powers; in a word, his Spiritual Evolution.

Now it so happens that as fast as one acquires spiritual understanding, his circumstances improve in every respect—his health, his temper, his happiness and his material surroundings rapidly and automatically change for the better. *Per contra*, a want of true understanding automatically and necessarily expresses itself in some sort of difficulty on the physical plane, culminating in sin, sickness, and death.

When people find themselves in any difficulty, should they have some glimmerings of spiritual truth, they realize, however dimly, that a way out is to be found along the path of spiritual enlightenment, and consequently they study books, consult friends in the movement, ask for treatment or guidance, or take whatever step appears to be appropriate at the moment. This is the natural and proper course to pursue, and, provided they understand what it is that they are doing, it is only a matter of time before their difficulties—their ill-health, their poverty, their trouble, whatever it is—must disappear. They are, in fact, seeking spiritual enlightenment; they are working for a change in consciousness; and one cannot seek for an improved consciousness without getting it, nor get it without making a demonstration. To know this is to have "come into Truth," to use the common phrase.

Misunderstanding and disappointment

arise when people mistake the teaching for some kind of elaborate conjuring trick. When a man supposes that by a wave of the hand, or the repetition of an incantation, his circumstances can be changed for the better without any corresponding change in his own mentality, he is doomed to disappointment. He has not come into Truth, and the Truth movement has nothing for him.

During the past few years a large number of people of all sorts have consulted me about their difficulties, and they easily divide themselves into those two groups. Some people, for instance, are in trouble owing to some very obvious defect in character, but are quite unwilling to overcome this defect, or even, in many cases, to acknowledge it; they wish to continue in their mistake and to have prosperity or happiness as well. Needless to say, for them there is no relief until they have suffered a little more, and have been punished sufficiently to make them do what is necessary. The man who drinks, for example, is certain to ruin his business,

and you cannot help him as long as he pre-
fers whiskey to prosperity. Of course, if he
is trying to give up whiskey, you can help
him to do so, and then all will be well, but
otherwise he will just have to go on suffering
until his lesson is learned. Other people
complain that they have no friends, cannot
keep servants, and that they live unhappy,
isolated lives; and a few minutes' conversa-
tion makes it obvious that there is an atro-
ciously bad temper there which has driven
everyone away. If such people are prepared to work to change themselves, the
road is clear; but until they are, there is
very little to be done for them.

Most of you who read this, however, will
be seeking the Truth in the right way, and
to seek the Truth in that spirit is really to
have come into Truth. "You would not have
sought Me had you not already found Me."
That being so, you should not allow yourself
to be worried or depressed merely because
the demonstration is delayed. If you have
sufficient understanding to believe in treat-

ment, you have sufficient understanding to know that it must be only a matter of time before you are out of the wood—and what does it really matter whether it is a little sooner or a little later. Any delay in getting results can only be due to one of two things: Either the mental cause of your difficulty is very deeply seated in your consciousness and is requiring a good deal of work; or else you are not yet working in the best way, and if this is so, again it will be only a matter of time before you find what is the best way for you. In other words, once you are on the Path there is no hurry. "Oh, but," says someone, "in my case there is the most urgent hurry, because unless I make my demonstration by Saturday the verdict of the Court will be given against me," or "my creditors will foreclose," or "I shall lose the boat," or what not. But the answer in Truth is still—*There is no hurry,* for the gates of hell shall never prevail. Let evil do its worst on Saturday; let the Court give its verdict; let the creditors strike their blow;

let the boat sail. When Monday comes, prayer will still put everything right, if you can get your realization, and if not on Monday, then Wednesday, or Friday, or the week after next. Time does not really matter, for prayer is creative, and will build the New Jerusalem for you anywhere, at any time, irrespective of what may have happened, just as soon as you can get your realization of Truth, Omnipresent Good—Emanuel, which is God with you. This is the New Jerusalem which comes down out of heaven like a bride adorned for her husband, and is independent of any conditions on the physical plane.

When you are in difficulties, look upon the overcoming of them as a great adventure. Resist the temptation to be tragic, to give way to self-pity or discouragement; and approach the problems as though you were an explorer seeking a path through Darkest Africa, or an Edison working to overcome difficulties in connection with a new invention. You know that there is a way out of any difficulty whatever, no matter what it may be, through the changing of your own consciousness by prayer. You know that by thus raising your consciousness any conceivable form of good that you can desire will be yours; and you know that nobody else can by any means hinder you from doing this when you really want to do it—relatives, customers, employers, the government, bad times, so-called—nothing can hinder you from the rebuilding of your own consciousness—and this rebuilding is the Great Adventure.

BY THE SAME AUTHOR

The prices are kept low in order to facilitate distribution by those desiring to spread the Truth.

The Sermon on the Mount—This book constitutes a complete course of instruction in Scientific Christianity $1.50

The Lord's Prayer—an interpretation. This gives a general outline of the whole teaching .... .25

The Garden of Allah—A Study in Treatment (Spiritual Key to Isaiah 35)................... .25

Your Heart's Desire .... .10

The Golden Key .... .10

The Yoga of Love.. .10

The Secret Place—a spiritual key to the 91st Psalm .... .20

The Wonder Child .... .10

The Presence—a spiritual treatment............ .05

The Word of Power .... .05

The Good Shepherd—a meditation on the 23rd Psalm .... .05

How to Prevent War.................................. .05

The Magic of Tithing .... .05

Dick Whittington—A study in Inspiration............ .05

Alter Your Life.. .05

The Bogey Man Under the Stairs—The final step in Metaphysics .... .05

Be Still—A Treatment against Fear (Spiritual Key to the 46th Psalm) .... .15

Truth Versus the Fool's Paradise .... .05

The Seven Day Mental Diet .... .10

The Golden Gate .... .05

Sowing and Reaping .... .05

The End of the World—The Zodiac and the Bible .... .20

The Historical Destiny of the United States —The Mystery of the American Money............ .50

The Everlasting Gates (Spiritual Key to the 24th Psalm—Demonstration Psalm)............ .15

Light and Salvation (Spiritual Key to the 27th Psalm) and No Results Without Prayer .15

(Postage Extra)

Box 128

Hotel Seville, New York, N. Y.

British Agents:

THE RALLY OFFICE

9 Percy St., London, W.I., England